The Invention of Poetry

Once upon a time Gary pitched in the
majors. He even has a bubble gum card to
prove it. Moon was once nominated for the
Nobel Prize for his poetry, but that was years
ago. Now they both live and drink in their
hideout from the world, a fleabag hotel.
Tonight the plan is to stay sober and to
create a poem of beauty and a joy forever.
But writing poetry requires a muse...

Paul Quarrington has won several awards for
his writing including The Stephen Leacock
Memorial Award for Humour for *King
Leary* in 1987, and the Governor General's
Award for *Whale Music* in 1989.

David Fox as Moon and Michael Hogan as Gary in the Canadian Stage Comapany/ Citadel Theatre production. Photo by Ed Ellis

The Invention of Poetry

Paul Quarrington

THE SUMMERHILL SEASON

The Summerhill Season is published by:
Summerhill Press Ltd., 52 Shaftesbury Avenue
Toronto, Ontario M4T 1A2

Distributed by:
University of Toronto Press, 5201 Dufferin Street
Downsview, Ontario M3H 5T8

General Editor: Michelle Maynes
Cover illustration: Dean McCallum
Author photo: Michael Burke

Printed and bound in Canada

Canadian Cataloguing in Publication Data

Quarrington, Paul
The invention of poetry

(The Summerhill Season)
A play.
ISBN 0-929091-31-0

I. Title. II. Series.

PS 8583.U33I68 1990   C812'.54   C90-095778-6
PR9199.3.Q37I68 1990

Enquiries regarding production rights should be directed to:
Peter Livingstone Associates, 92 King St. E., Ste. 311,
Toronto, Ontario M5C 2V8
Phone (416) 366-4486 FAX (416) 366-5060

For James Carroll

The Invention of Poetry premiered October 25, 1989 in Toronto as a co-production of the Citadel Theatre and The Canadian Stage Company, with the following cast:

MOON: David Fox

GARY: Michael Hogan

Director: Bill Glassco

The Characters

GARY Kennelly, late 30s, a failed baseball player

MOON, 50, a failed minor poet

The Setting

Night. The dead of winter. The New World Hotel. Right downtown. Cheap. Moon's room looks like all the other rooms, except that his has a bookcase.

GARY *Kennelly sits hunched over an old Remington typewriter, his fingers poised on the keyboard.* MOON *wanders about the room in his dressing gown, deep in thought.*

MOON: *We came from the hills and were heavengoing.*

(GARY *types that, very quickly.* MOON *is impressed*)

MOON: Where did you learn to do that?

GARY: I took secretarial sciences in high school.

MOON: Secretarial sciences. It sounds to me like the study of secretaries. How their complex internal plumbing operates, that sort of thing. Valuable stuff to know, Kennelly.

GARY: Yessir. The heavengoing?

MOON: *We came from the hills and were heavengoing.*

GARY: Is that two words, *heaven going*, or just one word all run together?

MOON: I do not care. I am working in the oral tradition. I am the last of the great Celtic bards and mystics, do not bother me with such trifles as whether or not heavengoing is one word or two.

GARY: Or hyphenated.

MOON: Always a possibility, Gary. I leave it in your capable hands. I could teach secretarial sciences. I've made it a lifelong study of mine. I've been peeking through bathroom doors, Kennelly. My Jesus. They do stuff in there makes nuclear physics look like child's play.

GARY: Shame on you.

MOON: Oh, yes. Shame on me.

GARY: The poem.

MOON: The poem. *We came from the hills and were heavengoing.* I need a drink.

GARY: No way for that, sonny-jim.

MOON: I'll pretend I didn't hear. I need a drink.

GARY: *We came from the hills and were heaven hyphen going.*

MOON: Give us just a small taste. A wee mooshy.

GARY: Go, man.

MOON: I know you've got some, Kennelly. You're a hopeless alcoholic.

GARY: Poetry.

MOON: You see, you see, that's just it. The poetry's come back. I can feel it in my bones. All it would take for it to come pouring out — like water from a fountain, my lad, like laughter from a schoolgirl — is a little taste.

GARY: Now this whole thing was your idea. You were going to say poetry, I was going to type it down. And you specifically mentioned there was to be no booze involved in the process.

MOON: I feel the bone-rattling of poetry! I need stuporifics.

GARY: You told me about Old Man Lawler and you said *there but for fortune* and you made me give my solemnest oath not to give you any.

MOON: I meant any *in quantity*. All I'm asking for is a sip. The tiniest mooshy. To wet my whistle.

GARY: Water.

MOON: Whiskey is water for the garden of my soul.

GARY: You'd rather get drunk than work on this here poem.

MOON: You are essentially a Barbary ape, Kennelly. This poetry is as foreign to you as the Dog Star Sirius. What's more, I don't believe this was my idea. And if it was, I certainly can't remember disallowing the woozle water. Now fetch us some of your rotgut!

GARY: We were sitting in the tavern downstairs. I said that I was thinking of hawking my typewriter. I only have it to write the occasional letter.

MOON: Every so often you'll pick out a "k" or an "h."

GARY: Letters to family.

MOON: I can see why you were thinking of pawning it.

GARY: Then you come up with this idea, you'll say poetry, I'll write it down. Or as you put it, you'll spew beauties, I'll skewer the buggers.

MOON: Ah! Now that has the ring of authenticity.

GARY: And I'll tell you what else, man, this is a nice line. *We came from the hills and were heavengoing.*

MOON: It does have a certain something. It's come back, Gary. Like an errant and unfaithful wife, the muse has returned. I shall welcome her into my embrace. All is forgiven.

GARY: Well then, go, man, go.

MOON: Stirring words. Go, man, go.

GARY: As Popeye Finlayson used to say, application plus dedication equals completion.

MOON: If I have not already disallowed the mention of Popeye Finlayson, Captain of the Stars —

GARY: Manager of the Komets. With a K. Most intelligent man I've ever met.

MOON: — I do so now. Banish the name from your lips.

GARY: Application. That's you deciding to make up a poem. Dedication is striving forward. Dedication is ix-nay to ooze-bay. Application plus dedication equals completion. Namely, one poem.

MOON: Come on, boozehound. I know you've got some.

GARY: Maybe I do. It's none of your concern. Application. Dedication.

MOON: You admit it!

GARY: Didn't you just get through calling me an alkie? And don't alkies usually have booze?

MOON: Just so. Produce it. Let's have a tug at the witch's tit, Kennelly. A wee mooshy. I release you from your vow. And it was very commendable the way you honoured it.

GARY: If I make a promise, I keep it. For the most part.

MOON: But in this particular case, it is not necessary for you to keep it. Just give me a bottle of goddamn booze.

GARY: Why don't you just calm down and write a little more poetry?

MOON: It's not that easy. I've a writer's block. It's frightening, laddy, the worst feeling imaginable. A thousand times worse than a failure to function sexually. Not that that's ever happened to me. My body has often been devoid of all sensibility, emptied of blood and humours, but Moon has somehow managed to pull out the living sausage and supply the cream to go with it.

GARY: (*snorts disdainfully despite himself*) Yeah, right.

MOON: What? What do you mean?

GARY: I go to secretarial science class and learn to type ninety words a minute — and get laughed at every day for my troubles — and then I end up here, and it must have been ten minutes ago that you said *we came from the hills and were heavengoing*. I could have typed that with my toes and been done by now.

MOON: Mooshy-mooshy.

GARY: Let's stop and approach this with a little common sense. As Popeye Finlayson used to say, the

uncommonest thing is ofttimes common sense.
We came from the hills. Fair enough. Therefore, we
are now at the bottom of them. Logic. What is at
the bottom of hills? I'll tell you what is. Trees.
What kind of trees? Might be, oh, weeping willow. There you go. Goddamn weeping willow
trees. What do they look like? They look kind of
weepy. Sad. And in the winter, they're green. So.
*We came from the hills and were heavengoing, and the
willows were weepy and wintergreen.*

MOON: It's laughable, Kennelly. It really is. A veritable
hoot. Give me a little taste and I'll show you a
master at work.

GARY: You told me what Old Man Lawler done. And
you said you'd taken a solemn vow never to
drink again.

MOON: I wasn't thinking properly.

GARY: And I think it's a fine thing when a man takes
the pledge.

MOON: This would explain why you've done it so
many times.

GARY: Different people got different problems.

MOON: What is that supposed to signify?

GARY: What washes for one fellow don't always wash
for the next.

MOON: Is this another piece of wisdom from Walleye Gustaffson? Words for hopeless alcoholics to live by?

GARY: Popeye Finlayson. And a fellow doesn't like to be all the time called a hopeless alcoholic and such.

MOON: I call a spade a spade. Produce the magic elixir.

GARY: And another thing. What the hell are you? I'm sitting here calm as the hair on a bear's butt, not even shaking a bit, and you are going nuts and screaming for booze, so what the Jesus H. Christ are you?

MOON: I am a poet.

GARY: Okay, then. I am a baseball player.

MOON: You haven't played baseball in years.

GARY: Haven't played in the *majors* in years. When was the last time you wrote a poem? Nineteen fifty-something?

MOON: I am the last of the great Celtic bards. You are a washed-up alcoholic baseball player. You barely deserve to be in the same room as me.

GARY: All right, old man. I'm gone. (*rises from the table*)

MOON: Wait. I spoke in haste.

GARY: I am not washed-up.

MOON: The mouth rushes forward, the brain dawdles behind.

GARY: I threw an imperfect game!

MOON: Yes, yes. I kn— you what?

GARY: Maybe I got a few problems, but don't we all? And I'm going to work them out, and then it's back into the world with me.

MOON: Yes, yes. My god, yes. You're a young man yet, Gary.

GARY: I feel good. Healthy.

MOON: You look in fine kith. A veritable Arnold Schwarzenegger.

GARY: Gezundheit. Well, you know, sure I've padded up some around the old belly, but that's just the booze. I cut the juice loose, I'll be in the trim. My arm is still as strong as ever she was.

> (MOON *has an idea. He suspects — correctly — that* GARY *is carrying a bottle of liquor in his jacket pocket.* GARY *has discarded his jacket over in a corner.* MOON *thinks that if he can distract* GARY *— and distracting* GARY *is often a fairly easy task — he can sneak over and claim this prize)*

MOON: I am intrigued by your career as a baseball player. What exactly were you?

GARY: Kansas City Royal. Although mostly I was with the Komets, with a K, which is part of the Royal system. Played out of a town in Georgia named Keever. Sherman marched through Keever. I was also a Blue Jay, a Cardinal and briefly a Mudhen. Then I ended up here, where I was for one whole game a member of the Tarpits.

What are you doing?

> (MOON *has neared the goal, but at* GARY's *question he spins around quickly*)

MOON: These transmogrifications are fascinating, but you have misunderstood the thrust of my query. What rosterial function did you fulfill?

GARY: What position, you mean?

MOON: Exactly that.

> (GARY *begins to answer, and* MOON *begins to sneak up on the jacket*)

GARY: Pitcher. Long relief. Mind you, when I first came up there was talk I'd be a starter. I was a starter for the Komets. But then I had a few bad games. Hey, it's like Popeye Finlayson said, many a fragrant flower has sprouted from a cracked seed.

(MOON *has extracted a bottle from* GARY's
*jacket and is clandestinely trying to take a
sip*)

GARY: You won't like it, Moon. It's rye.

MOON: Canadian horse-piss.

(MOON *drinks*)

MOON: I'll die a young man.

GARY: Gonna write some more poetry?

MOON: *We came from the hills and were heavengoing,
and...the trees were weepy and wintergreen.*

GARY: *Willows* were weepy.

MOON: Got that?

GARY: Got it. (*types*)

MOON: Care for a wee mooshy?

GARY: Give it over.

MOON: This really is fascinating stuff. Long relief.
Sounds so pleasant. Sounds like very gratifying
employment. What do you do? *Long relief.* What
exactly is long relief?

GARY: Well, they call for long relief when the shit is
tumbling from the sky. The starter has screwed
things up but good. Usually when I'd come in,
we'd already be down four, five runs. Men on
base. Nobody out. Not a good situation, Moon.

MOON: Yes, but I'm sure you were stalwart and true and did whatever it is you had to do. Here's what I'm wondering, though, Kennelly. If you were long relief, was there also a player referred to as *brief relief*?

GARY: Short relief. The glory boy. See, Kennelly goes in there and sweats like a stuck pig. Maybe I've given up a couple of runs, nothing too serious. Meantime the boys have started hitting. The Royals always could hit them a few. So maybe we might take the lead, five-four or something, top of the eighth, and then they bring in the kid with the blonde hair and the big dick and the ninety-five miles per hour on his change-up and he whiffs them, bing-bing-bing.

MOON: Bing-bing-bing. I'm sure you were a fine baseballer, Gary.

> (MOON *drinks and wanders about the room.*
> GARY *reaches into his back pocket for his*
> *wallet, extracts an old and battered bubble*
> *gum card which he hands to* MOON)

GARY: Lookee. I found this the other day. I'd stuck it in my...in a book.

MOON: Reading books again, young man? Shame on you. Well, well. A fine likeness.

GARY: I used to have a crewcut.

David Fox as Moon and Michael Hogan as Gary in the Citadel Theatre/
Canadian Stage Company Production. Photo by Ed Ellis.

MOON: It's very neat, Gary.

GARY: It's easy to manage, a crewcut. Just get up in the morning, doesn't need combing or anything.

MOON: I should imagine.

> (MOON *drinks again and flips the card over,*
> *examining the other side*)

MOON: Personal FAX. What does that mean, F-A-X?

GARY: Personal facts. Stats and shit.

MOON: Let me see. B—

GARY: That's B for born.

MOON: Oh, I see. How clever. Saved them from having the remaining three letters. B, 1951, Coffeyville, Mo. M-O?

GARY: Missouri. That's where the Dalton Gang got shot up. Coffeyville, Missouri.

MOON: Thereupon follows a series of numbers.

GARY: Wins, losses, E.R.A.

MOON: Hmm! I'm sure these numbers are exemplary. I've rarely seen such attractive numbers. Wait. There's still more personal F-A-X. *Gary is married to wife Jocelyn and the proud father of twin girls.*

GARY: Give it back.

MOON: Certainly. I'm afraid I don't have any of mine around the place, they're quite the collector's item.

GARY: What's this now?

MOON: My card from Famous Poet's Chewing Gum. It's got a photograph of myself on the front, made back in the days when I sported an easy-to-manage crewcut. Then on the back my B-place is cited, Hay on Wye, Hereford and Worcester. H on W, H and W. Thereupon ensues my stats and so forth. Personal FAX. *Moon has been married several times and is the proud father of more horrid mewling infants than he can count.*

GARY: Come on, now. I may not know much, but I know this. A daddy loves his babies.

MOON: May I come live in your little world with you? Everything seems so nice.

GARY: Huh?

MOON: My daddy didn't love his babies. My daddy used to beat his babies.

GARY: He never.

MOON: Well, some loutish creature most certainly did, and he bore the father a stunning resemblance.

GARY: I don't know, man.

MOON: I've shaken Kennelly to the very essence of his being. Here, lad, have some of this Canadian why whiskey.

> (GARY *accepts the bottle and drinks, still a little lost in thought*)

Just mind you don't get so drunk you can't type. The poetry's about to come.

GARY: I don't get drunk. I maintain. There's a big difference.

MOON: Yes, yes.

GARY: Probably you weren't actually a baby. A fellow would never hit a baby.

MOON: No, no, certainly not. He waited until I was sixteen months, old enough to defend myself.

GARY: One time when I was about fifteen my daddy tried to lay a beating on me.

MOON: And?

GARY: And he wished he hadn't of.

MOON: I've a similar anecdote. The old pater comes in one night, outrageously woofled, and he starts in on mother. I was sitting in the corner reading poetry. Keats, the collected poems, with selected letters, a thick leatherbound volume. I coldcocked

him with it, my friend. Me and Johnny Keats laid
out the blackguard on his duff.

GARY: You didn't.

MOON: True story, mate. And then — then mother gets
up and slaps me. Well, that's when I realized that
men are fools and women are mad. We don't
stand a chance, Kennelly. Give us the hooch. Let
us drink, for all about is naught but ruin and
desolation.

GARY: You got what Popeye called a negative attitude.

MOON: Good old Popeye. Here's to him, may our
paths never cross.

GARY: Take Popeye. He was called Popeye because he
only had one eye, and the other one was just an
empty socket that he used to keep all squinted
up, so he looked like this. (*makes a face*) Ugly man.
Had hair all over his body. Skin was blotchy. One
leg about a foot shorter than the other. But he had
a positive attitude!

MOON: Oh, god.

GARY: It's like one time his car was stolen. Man say,
Popeye, your car just disappeared. And old
Popeye says, lucky for me I wasn't in it at the
time, or I would have disappeared, too. Get it?

MOON: The mysteries of Popeye's wisdom are not entirely lost upon me, Kennelly.

GARY: Negative thinking creates physical limitations. The secret is having a positive attitude.

MOON: Yes, yes. That's how you got where you are today.

GARY: This is just a temporary thing. I got a little problem, namely that stuff right there which would you please hand over, but I think I've got it just about licked. Then maybe I'll head down to Florida and play a little winter ball. But look, I'm being realistic. I know I'm too old for the show, but if I could get hitched up with a team, even single-A, I could make one hell of a pitching coach. Then one day I might even manage a team. Do good in single-A through triple-A — success must come on all levels, as Popeye used to say — I may even manage in the majors. You never know. My point is, I ain't sticking around this fleabag hotel all my life.

MOON: I imagine they have cute matching names. April and May. Tuesday and Wednesday. Fric and Frac.

GARY: Who's this? My daughters?

MOON: The twin girls, of which you are so proud.

GARY: Melody and Melanie.

MOON: I see.

GARY: Melanie died, though, when she was seven.

MOON: Did I ask?

GARY: I'm just saying.

MOON: Keep that sort of thing to yourself. Don't volunteer information.

GARY: I thought you might be interested.

MOON: I'm not. Got it? I'm not interested in the slightest.

GARY: (*shrugs, drinks, looks at the paper in the typewriter*) Hey, now. We done bogged down again.

(MOON *relieves* GARY *of the bottle*)

MOON: I was going great guns, by Jesus, I was spouting crude beauty, lad, and then you talk about these things which don't concern me in the least and I lose my train of thought.

GARY: I'm sorry.

MOON: Read for me what we have thus far.

GARY: *We came from the hills and were heavengoing, and the willows were weepy and wintergreen.*

MOON: Highly alliterative that. One of my trademarks. Did you notice, Garibaldi? Hills, heaven. Weepy, winter, willows. The crickets will start to chirp.

MOON: (*continued*) Yes, the little-brained literary crickets will have me on that, saying that I've made scant progress since I published *The Rowdy Heavens*. Bugger the bastards, that's what I say. Bugger the boogerish bastards.

GARY: Hey, my daddy was alliterative.

MOON: Watch now. I'll show you how it's done.

We came from the hills and were heavengoing and the willows were weepy and wintergreen.

And... (*takes a drink*)

*And the morning...*type away, boy...*the morning caught us...um, unfledged, keening...*

GARY: Go, man, go.

MOON: Bogged down, I'm afraid.

GARY: What the hell is *unfledged*?

MOON: Without feathers, my lad.

GARY: Yeah?

MOON: It's a poetic way to say with our balls hanging out. *The morning caught us, unfledged, keening.* That's all right.

GARY: Damn nice, I'd say.

MOON: Did you notice the double meaning of the word *keening*?

GARY: I'll tell you the truth, pardner, I never noticed the single meaning.

MOON: Ah. Care for a wee mooshy?

GARY: Yo.

> (GARY *takes the bottle, drinks.* MOON *goes over and sits on the bed wearily.* GARY *watches him for awhile in silence*)

GARY: What about the poetry, Moon?

MOON: I am ruminating. I am sifting through my innards. I get this stuff from deep dark holes, Gary. It's not like I pluck it from supermarket shelves.

GARY: Uh-yeah.

> (*There is silence for a bit*)

GARY: Hey, man. I was talking to Kristal yesterday.

MOON: Kristal of the purple toenails? Kristal of the rouged nipples? Kristal of the coiffed pubis? In short, Kristal the whore?

GARY: Yeah. And she was saying how one night last week —

MOON: Hey, alkie! You're going to drink all the booze!

GARY: I got— (*falls abruptly silent*)

MOON: You got?

GARY: Let me ask about this thing with Kristal.

MOON: You got another bottle?

GARY: Well, now, I do and I don't.

MOON: No philosophical niceties. Scamper across to
   your room and fetch it.

GARY: Now, the thing of it is, tomorrow is Sunday.

MOON: The Sabbath. A day of contemplative pursuit.
   You won't need the hooch.

GARY: Yeah, but, if we drink both of the bottles today,
   then I sure as shit *will* need the other bottle tomorrow, and if I already drank it, then I'm gonna
   be in trouble.

MOON: For god's sake, be a man, Kennelly. Don't kow-
   tow to these weaknesses.

GARY: If I drink too much now, I won't be maintaining.
   And tomorrow I won't be able to maintain at all.

MOON: You jellyfish. You spineless sniveller.

GARY: Yeah, well, at least I can still fuck occasionally,
   which is more than what I hear about you.

MOON: What?

GARY: I was talking to Kristal.

MOON: It's time for violence. I'm about to get violent.
   I'm going to break things, Kennelly, over your

thick skull. Wait, wait! Where's Johnny Keats? (*rushes to his bookcase and starts searching*)

Death by poetry. The skull crushed by the collected poems of that beautiful consumptive boy. Here it is! Prepare to die, Kennelly!

GARY: Come on at me, old man. I'll punch your teeth so far down your throat you'll have to stick your toothbrush up your butt.

MOON: (*raises the book, rushes forward — stops abruptly*) Hold on. I've just had a thought. You — trusting, wide-eyed simpleton that you are — never lock your door.

GARY: I got nothing worth stealing.

(MOON *hands* GARY *the volume of poetry*)

MOON: Educate yourself.

(MOON *leaves the room.* GARY *scowls, thumbs through the book of poetry. A few moments later* MOON *returns, a bottle in one hand, a Bible in the other*)

Irish whiskey! Very fancy, Gary.

GARY: I thought maybe we'd drink it tomorrow and celebrate the fact that you'd written a poem.

MOON: This is what Billy Yeats drank. He'd drink this and then he'd write the loveliest damn poetry the world has ever heard. I knew him, of course. I was just a boy. I pissed on his knee. I knew them all, Kennelly. I am the last of them. I knew Brendan. I knew Dylan. I had his wife, you know. Good old Caitlin Thomas. Dylan, poor boy, was impotent. I was but seventeen and had jism coming out my ears. (*drinks deeply*)

And look what else was in your room. The Holy Bibble. What are you doing, Kennelly, looking for loopholes?

GARY: Nothing wrong with reading scripture.

MOON: Perhaps you have been born again, again?

GARY: No, sir. It's just that occasionally I enjoy looking at the Bible.

MOON: There's some fine poetry in here. *Thy lips are like a thread of scarlet, and thy speech is comely. Thy two breasts are like two young roes that are twins, which feed among the lilies.* Bit heavy-handed. Rather frightening when you think about it, young bucks gallavanting across the poor dolly's chest.

GARY: Do you believe in God, Moon?

MOON: That's not the sort of thing one asks.

GARY: Where'd you get all these rules for talking, anyway? We're just two guys in a room, what does it matter?

MOON: No. No. I don't believe in God.

GARY: Yeah?

MOON: I've responded.

GARY: You don't just say yes or no.

MOON: Now you're the one with the rules.

GARY: It's not a rule. But if a fellow says he doesn't believe in God, he can't just leave it hanging there.

MOON: I don't feel up to bandying about bits of theology.

GARY: I believe in God. I wish I didn't. I —

MOON: Fair enough, lad.

GARY: I can explain.

MOON: I seek no explanation.

GARY: Well, suppose I don't give a good god damn what you seek, fat man? I can say whatever I want.

MOON: You believe in God, but it troubles you to the quick because He's such a big meany.

GARY: I can give you an example.

MOON: It's old hat, mate. Look, it's in the book. *Come, behold the works of the Lord, what desolation he hath made in the earth. He breaketh the bow and cutteth the spear in sunder; he burneth the chariot in fire.*

GARY: I don't think you read that, Moon. I think you knew it.

> (MOON *closes the book, sets it down. He tilts the bottle to his mouth*)

Let's have some of that Irish stuff over here.

MOON: You finish up that Canadian horse-piss.

GARY: I bought the both of them.

MOON: You shouldn't mix your alcoholic beverages so freely. That's what causes drunkeness.

GARY: I don't get drunk. I maintain.

MOON: Well, I do. I get drunk. I am a drunkard. You are an alcoholic, I am a drunkard. The difference being, I don't have to go to all those damn meetings.

GARY: I go to the meetings because I want to beat this thing.

MOON: Stop drinking. Don't be so lily-livered.

GARY: Thank you, Mister Women's Christian Temperance Union. You sound like Jocelyn. You got no idea what it's like.

MOON: And I'll do you this further favour, because I know how serious you are about stopping. I'll consume all your liquor for you.

GARY: You should come to a few meetings.

MOON: Not for me, Gary. I don't like this *I am a lowly, lorn shebeener* attitude. Did you have to tell them about all the many horrid things you've done? Waking up in Cincinnati with a mouthful of dung beside a pox-ridden harridan with no teeth and a knife in her back?

GARY: One time I did get up.

MOON: Oh, nay, never say it.

GARY: What happens is, you stand up and say, "My name is Gary, and I am an alcoholic." And then everybody says, all together they say, "Hi Gary!"

MOON: How very summer-camp of them.

GARY: So...I didn't say my right name.

MOON: Took the anonymous aspect one step further, did you?

GARY: I said my name was Mickey. "My name is Mickey, and I am an alcoholic." And they all went, "Hi, Mickey!"

> (*They laugh.* GARY *is more amused by* MOON's *reaction than by the little joke itself.* MOON *laughs until he starts coughing — he hacks for a while and then lights a cigarette*)

I didn't think you'd know about that show, The Mickey Mouse Club, I mean.

MOON: Oh, yes. I was quite a fan. I used to watch it with my boy Hamish.

GARY: Is Hamish the one who — ?

MOON: (*startled*) Have I mentioned Hamish?

GARY: Couple times.

MOON: Into my cups, was I? I'm sorry, Gary.

GARY: It's nothing to be sorry about.

MOON: Oh, certainly it is.

GARY: Quite the little piano player, was he?

MOON: Yes. He played the piano. How — ?

GARY: Sometimes it helps, you know, to remember things like that. You don't have to remember everything, but something like piano music, that might help.

MOON: It doesn't help to remember anything.

GARY: Sure it does.

MOON: Mind your own business, Kennelly.

GARY: It's all you talk to me about when you're pissed. I kind of figure it is my business.

MOON: I talk about Hamish, do I?

GARY: And there's nothing wrong with that.

MOON: I am a poet! The last of the great Celtic bards. My heart is as black and as full as the cosmos. And here you depict me like an old...*drunk*. A maudlin old drunk spilling tears into his beer. It's not so. You're lying, aren't you?

GARY: Maybe we should get back to work.

MOON: Yes! Certainly. Read me what I have created thus far.

GARY: *We came from the hills and were heavengoing, and the willows were weepy and wintergreen. The morning caught us, unfledged, keening...* That's it.

MOON: That's all? You must have missed something. I've been spouting the old poetry like nobody's business.

GARY: Seems like it to me, too, but this is all we've got.

MOON: I've tackled the big one, mate, I can see that. This is no ode to pussy or pancakes. The subject here is life itself. Birth, you see, is what I've just described. Born into this wintry vale, unfledged, keening — double meaning there, laddy, think about it — and now we must move on to another stage of life. One more tug at the witch's nipple. We must start thinking form. That's the part you plebs never understand, Kennelly. You think it's all blood and guts, but no. (*taps his forehead*)

There's quite a bit of this in the old poetry. Form.
Architectonics. Anyone can bung a bunch of
words onto a piece of paper, but it's like raping a
virgin. I think what I want is another *ee* sound,
possibly a rhyme for *going. Boing.* Perhaps not.
You see, Kennelly? Poet at work. Here we go
then. *The morning caught us, unfledged, keening,*
grieving, *earthbound and stumble-toed.* There.
Fucking beauty. Slipped out like a silken shit.
Poetry.

GARY: Hot damn.

MOON: I've done it. I've created some goddamn poetry! I'm goose-tingled, Gary. Horripilated! I'm
feather-headed!

GARY: Keep it going.

MOON: Yes, yes. Um…the sun. Not the sun. That's
Ibsen. Forget the sun. The Moon. Never mind the
silly moon. Forget all celestial orbs. Tits! No. I'm
losing it, son. Help me.

GARY: The wind.

MOON: Yes, yes, of course, the wind. A zephyr. Ethereal. The wind of…

GARY: Wonder. Alliterative. Go, man, go.

MOON: The wind of will! Yes, the wind of will, the
dust of tears…

GARY: (*begins to type quickly*) Whoo-boy! Go!

MOON: *The wind of will, the dust of tears, the sacrament of sorrow...*

GARY: Tomorrow.

MOON: What?

GARY: *Tomorrow* rhymes with *sorrow*.

MOON: Does it indeed?

GARY: Say what?

MOON: Kennelly, you have thrown a spanner into the works. You have erected a huge stop sign and the automobile of creative genius has screeched to a halt.

GARY: I was just saying a rhyme for you.

MOON: It's hard to believe that the world created such men as Keats, Coleridge and Shelley, because I know for a fact that they were all on their tod. Shelley, for example, although possessed of a hideously ugly wife — and nothing creates the poetic impulse so much as an intimacy with ugliness — Shelley was bereft of the company of a washed-up alcoholic baseball player who would call out grade-two style rhymings for him. How Percy Bysshe managed to produce any work at all under those circumstances is a complete bafflement.

GARY: Sorry. I got caught up. The word *tomorrow* just kind of jumped into my head.

MOON: I've lost it.

GARY: *The wind of will, the dust of tears, the sacrament of sorrow* —

MOON: No, no. I mean I've lost it. The poetry.

GARY: Positive attitude.

MOON: Fuck Popeye Finlayson! Positive attitude? We live at Pluto's Hideaway. This is the Gehenna Hotel, mate. Gary, this is the end of the bleeding rope.

GARY: I'm sure there's worse places.

MOON: Have you noticed the sign downstairs? Do you know what the big selling point at this place is? Ashtrays In Every Room! Of course. There must needs be ashtrays in this lake of fire and brimstone.

GARY: Look. It's no sin for a fellow to fall down on his luck, and then maybe he can't afford, you know, a condo in Waikiki, but we got a roof over our heads, beds to lay in…

MOON: I wouldn't mind, except that it's gone.

GARY: What's this now?

MOON: The poetry. You see before you the saddest of sights, a poet with no poetry left inside.

GARY: Goddamn, man. Everybody's got poetry in him. Only difference with a poet is a poet knows how to get the damn stuff out.

MOON: I'm a hopeless alkie, I can see that now. Starting tomorrow it's tea and mineral water for me.

GARY: Yeah, you can join the Club Soda. But hey, maybe you could start on that tea and mineral water now, you know. I'm gonna need that stuff tomorrow.

MOON: Why am I drunk? Didn't I make you promise not to give me any? You, of all people, should know better than to give alcohol to a hopeless alkie. I mean, have they never mentioned that at any of the meetings? Now you see me, a pitiful drunkard. A hopeless alkie. I've been noticing the effects, don't think I haven't. A puffiness beneath the eyes. The eyes themselves like stones. My nose is grog-blossomed, my belly distended like a Biafran orphan's. I shit blood and I piss razors. I suppose Kristal the trollop told you how my prowess mysteriously deserted me? It was the drink. The mare's piss robbed me of my marrow.

GARY: What Kristal said was, you made her look into your eyes. For an hour. You made her kneel in front of you and look into your eyes.

MOON: The drink, the drink. It's appalling what the drink can do.

GARY: Hell, yes. When you told me about Mr. Lawler, I thought, jeez.

MOON: How nicely put. Jeez.

GARY: He couldn't have been that old. Sixty-something.

MOON: And do you know, lad, just the other day Lawler was telling me he was moving to Florida. The land of Ponce de Leon.

GARY: They got quite a few ponces down there in Florida.

MOON: Here's something I find very interesting. Lawler never turned off his little black-and-white television set. Left the thing on and dangled in front of it. And I wonder if it all meant so little to him that it didn't even deserve the small dignity of turning the telly off. Or, perhaps, in some strange way he wanted a witness. I don't know.

GARY: He probably just forgot about it.

MOON: There are suicides and then there are suicides. For example, one of my wives attempted it, rather half-heartedly I must say, a handful of Sleep-eaze or something. On the other hand, you have people who off themselves with relish and enthusiasm. I may have mentioned my son Hamish once or twice.

GARY: My daughter caught leukemia.

MOON: I want no further information concerning your daughter. And what's more, one doesn't catch leukemia. One is caught by leukemia. I believe leukemia favours the flying leg-lock tackle.

GARY: I was just saying what happened.

MOON: Have you ever thought about it, Garibaldi? Suicide?

GARY: That's not the sort of thing —

MOON: Hmm?

GARY: Well, no. Not really.

MOON: The way to do it, I understand, is to fall asleep in the snow. Get dead-drunk and wander outside in the dead of winter, and just have a little kip. A night like tonight seems perfect. Simply get drunk and fall asleep in the lovely white snow.

GARY: I never really gave it any thought at all. Now, how about we get back to work on the poem?

MOON: Well, I hope Lawler's passage was a peaceful one. They say that those that have gone on before come to greet you. That must be very wonderful, don't you think, Gary?

GARY: I think you are drunk and getting drunker. Now make some poetry.

MOON: I am drunk. It's true. You made a solemn oath not to give me liquor, yet here I am, pissed. Have some of this Irish whiskey, laddy-buck. That Canadian swill will rot your teeth and cause your nipples to fall off.

GARY: Thanks, pard.

MOON: Maintaining?

GARY: Maintaining.

MOON: As soon as that's gone, that's it for me. I'm a hopeless alkie, I can see that now.

GARY: Me, too, I guess.

MOON: You are, son, it's true. Hopeless.

GARY: I wouldn't necessarily say hopeless. Hey, it's like Popeye used to say: Give a man in the desert a bucket and the situation is no longer hopeless.

MOON: What a tiresome old fart Popeye is.

GARY: Finest baseball mind I've ever encountered. Ugly man, though.

MOON: And, Popeye's pithiness notwithstanding, I would and will continue to say hopeless.

GARY: Why don't you work it into the poem?

MOON: In time.

GARY: You're bogging down. Let's put in the word hopeless.

MOON: I want to put it in again and again. I want the next line to be *hopeless, hopeless, hopeless.* But...but that's too many. Don't hit them over the head, Kennelly. Scratch their balls, caress their pussies, but never bludgeon them with words. So, now, ahem... Hopeless. *Helpless.* You see that tiny transmogrification? I love that sort of shit. *Hopeless, helpless* — internal rhyme coming up, I'm mad for internal rhymes — *guessing* — yes — *guessing the wind's true tack.* There. Fucking poetry.

(GARY *types away*)

Came up like satin vomit.

GARY: Well done, Moon.

MOON: You don't suppose it's finished?

GARY: The poem?

MOON: That very thing.

GARY: I don't know, man. Seems awful short.

MOON: Who said we were creating an epic? There's nothing wrong with a small, well-crafted piece of work.

GARY: Ends kind of all of a sudden.

MOON: Oh, become a cricket have we?

GARY: She rolls along real nice and then runs out of steam.

MOON: So do all things, my lad. Entrapped by entropy.

GARY: Say now! (*begins to type*) There's some goddamn poetry!

MOON: Stop! Cease this instant, you scabrous lout!

GARY: *Entrapped by entropy.* I just know that is damn fine poetry, because I got no idea what it means. I just like the sound of the booger. *Entrapped by entropy.*

MOON: It does have a ring, doesn't it?

GARY: Sure. Now we're over the hump.

MOON: Alright. Let me take a look at this pitiful little cripple. Gary, I'm going to dedicate this piece to the memory of Mr. Lawler.

GARY: I thought you weren't too fond of the man.

MOON: He was a bit idiosyncratic.

GARY: You used to call him a mouseturd.

MOON: Yes, well, even mouseturds deserve to get the occasional bit of poetry dedicated to them, Kennelly.

GARY: I suppose.

MOON: Tomorrow, I'm off the drink forever. I may even attend some of those meetings. What's the atmosphere like?

GARY: It is goddamn smoky. Those people may have licked booze, but cigarettes is kicking the piss out of them.

MOON: Doesn't sound the thing for me.

GARY: You get off the juice, those meetings will help you a lot. It's the getting off that's tough.

MOON: Not for a man of my character. I'll simply cast it aside like so much dross. I'll get back my youth and vitality. Then you'll see poetry, mate. Then the crude beauty will bubble up like a geyser. I'll spray the world with it. You can't drink and work, lad. That much I've discovered. Poetry demands finely tuned sensibilities.

GARY: So does throwing a curve. A couple of beers and that curveball would straighten out so that even the batboy could hit it out of the park.

MOON: You wouldn't drink before a game, would you?

GARY: See, the problem with being long relief is that you never know when they might need you. A starter, a starter gets told he's going to pitch Thursday, and then he soaks it up on Tuesday,

gets sober on Wednesday and he's as good as
new by Thursday. I was always at the park, wondering if I was going to pitch that day. And we
might be up by three runs, so I'd think, okay, one
beer. And I'd scoot into the clubhouse. And then
we might go up by five runs. Another beer.
Maybe it'd get to the fourth, fifth inning, I'd
think, no work for me today, so glug-glug-glug,
then the starter would throw a series of balloons,
bang, bang, bang, all of a sudden they're calling
for the Kid.

MOON: And your curveball would straighten out.

GARY: Straighten out like my daddy's dick when he
saw my ma bended over the bathtub.

MOON: Ha! Now that is poetry.

GARY: It is?

MOON: Indeed.

GARY: How about that. Hey, you know what else,
Moon? Words keep popping into my head. Like
that *tomorrow*. Just popped into my head.

MOON: Take care you don't get the poetry bug, boy. It
will destroy your life. Fully ninety percent of all
poets end up alcoholic, mentally unbalanced and
suicidal. And the remaining ten percent write
shit.

GARY: I hear you, man.

MOON: *And mighty poets in their misery dead.*

GARY: (*he types*) Hey, hey.

MOON: Whoa-up, Kennelly. I'm afraid I was merely reminded of the words of that splay-footed, sister-fucking sissy Willy Wordsworth.

GARY: Oh.

MOON: And this he said likewise:
Oh, many are the poets that are sown
by nature; men endowed with highest gifts
the vision and the faculty divine:
Yet wanting the accomplishment of verse.

GARY: I should read some of those dudes.

MOON: By all means. Read some of those dudes.

GARY: You seem partial to this fellow here.

MOON: Keats! The lovely lad, frail and tubercular, coughing up his youth and beauty. Dead at twenty-six, Kennelly.

GARY: (*reading from the volume*) *A thing of beauty is a joy forever. Its loveliness increases.*

MOON: *It will never*
pass into nothingness; but still will keep
a bower quiet for us, and a sleep
full of sweet dreams, and health, and quiet breathing.

GARY: Damned nice.

MOON: Damned nice.

GARY: Let's write us a poem, Moon. A thing of frigging beauty and a joy forever.

MOON: Uh-oh. You're lost.

GARY: See now, looking at this thing here, I can see where you're coming from. Birth and all. But then you get older. And I reckon we're right about at the point of this thing where love rears its ugly head.

MOON: (*races away, pretending to be mortally afraid*) Oh, no! Kennelly has become poetical and wants to write about love!

GARY: What else you gonna write about?

MOON: Anything else. Teeth. Write about tractor-trailers. Write about the Kansas City Royals.

GARY: Well, I think one time I might write a poem about the Royals. But you started this poem here. And looking at it, I can't help thinking that it's time for love to enter the picture. Think about it.

MOON: This is what maddens the poets, what drives them to drink and to cold, cold graves. This impulse to write about something that simply does not exist.

GARY: You don't believe that, Moon.

MOON: You don't know what I do and don't believe.

GARY: Don't be so sure.

MOON: I have never been in love, Kennelly. I have been pussy-whipped and fuck-foundered. I have been cunt-struck and snatch-stayed. But I have never been in love.

GARY: How many times you been married?

MOON: God, who knows? Four times? Five times? Something along those lines.

GARY: And you weren't in love with a one of them?

MOON: I know what I'm supposed to say. The first one. The one that died. Piss on that!

GARY: She died?

MOON: I'm sorry, Kennelly.

GARY: I know where you're coming from, man. My daughter —

MOON: I suppose you've been in love countless times? I suppose every spring fills you with a burgeoning and giddy joy?

GARY: I've been in love exactly once. But it was love.

MOON: Yes, yes. And here you are in a palatial honeymoon suite with your fair Juliet blowing kisses from a bubble bath.

GARY: I got married too young, that was my mistake. Had the twins when I was nineteen. Nineteen years old, got a wife, two kids and a curveball that straightened out. Quite the hand God dealt me.

MOON: There! Now you've said God! Words such as love and God are slipping through your lips. The poetry is done, Kennelly. Pack up that instrument of torture and clear out.

GARY: What do you mean, *torture*?

MOON: You wouldn't understand. This is torture. This is pulling teeth that have roots reaching to my testes. When I was young, when I was your age, I could slap down the old poetry like no one. I was all alone in the universe. You wouldn't understand.

GARY: Sure I would.

MOON: Oh, would you?

GARY: Yeah. I threw an imperfect game, didn't I?

MOON: You've used this strange and elliptical phrase before. What in god's name do you mean?

GARY: I mean that the game wasn't perfect.

MOON: Oh, I see. In that case, what a concise and telling phrase it is.

GARY: Could have been, though. Could have been. Listen up. Funnily enough, it was Friday the thirteenth. Hot day in August. Kind of day when no one feels like doing anything. But they had a ballgame on, Komets versus the Kisamee Astros. Popeye gives me the nod. Truth of the matter is, I didn't really feel too good. I was a bit hungover. I was a lot hungover. Melanie had only died a couple months before —

(MOON *goes to interrupt*)

Hey, you don't have to listen, Moon. My girl died. It's not volunteered information or any other of your nonsense. It is what the fuck happened.

MOON: Carry on. The ballgame.

GARY: I told Popeye I wasn't up to it. And Popeye said, he said, what is the leper as he walks through the Holy Land?

MOON: Hold on.

GARY: And likewise what is the holy man who dwells among the lepers?

MOON: Wait up, Kennelly. It won't do.

GARY: That Popeye. What a character.

MOON: My goodness, yes. Ugly man, though.

GARY: Damn ugly.

So anyway, I started warming up. The country
fair was set up, you know, beside the park. The
air was full of sounds and smells. Laughing. Hey,
girl in row three there smiling at me. Wearing a
little halter-top. Just smiling, nothing shy about it.
I'm married, well, you got to understand, Moon, I
was a faithful husband and all, but after Melanie
died, there was sometimes when…girl sitting in
row three came from another place, you understand, where everyone was healthy and no one
had leukemia…

MOON: You digress.

GARY: All I'm saying is, I see row three smiling at me
and I think *all right*. I start warming up. My arm
gets good. I get comfortable. Game starts. I got all
my pitches working, Moon. Fast ball. Curve.
Sinker. Change-up like an old lady walking to
church. Girl in row three smiling at me. You
know what I notice about her, Moon? She's cross-
eyed. Not enough to make her look dopey, her
eyes are just a little bit skewed. Well, you see a
cross-eyed woman in your home park, that's a
fine and wonderful portent. Popeye says it means
they're watching the game in Heaven.

The Astros are falling like dead men. They're just

looking at my stuff. It's like they can't believe I'm doing it. It's like, what the fuck happened to Kennelly? And that's what I'm thinking, too, you know, what in the world is going on? They go one, two, three. One, two, three. One, two, three. Between innings I sit in the dugout. I'm thinking, yeah, I got a hold of it this time. I ain't gonna let go.

MOON: Cross-eyed girl in row three. The very air swims with augury.

GARY: Still smiling, my man. Meanwhile, Fergie cracks a solo sometime in the fifth. I tell the boys, thank you, kindly, that's all I'll need. Seventh inning. I'm even faster. I'm shaving corners like the girls before bikini season. One, two, three. Eighth inning — I haven't even thought it yet, Moon.

MOON: Haven't thought — ?

GARY: The P-word. Don't even think it. So, the eighth inning. They start throwing pinch hitters at me. Monk Grabowski. He goes for a low ball, pops it up to shallow centre field. One, two, three. Between innings. I smile at row three. Don't think the P-word, just don't think it, Kennelly. Just feel comfortable. You finally belong on this motherfucking godforsaken sumbitching planet.

Ninth inning. The word has spread through the

fairgrounds, you know, kid over in the ballpark got himself a P-word game going on. People everywhere. That's alright. That's alright, I'm not nervous. Hello, row three. Shine up your headlights, sister, I'll be taking a long drive in just a while. Who we got here? Ah. Santiago. Mooey regretto, amigo. Eat this. Pops it up, second base man swallows it like mammy's milk. One. Roid Mulgrew. Leads the leagues in homers. I don't care, I throw him fast and clean and in the zone, just daring him to hit a ball. And I'm not worried, in fact, all this time I'm thinking, what in the hell kind of name is *Roid*? Roid goes fishing, low ball with otherworldly stuff on it. So. Two. One man to go. I think it. I think, Gary, my son, you got a perfect game going on.

MOON: You thought the P-word? For shame.

GARY: You don't got to tell me, man. Stupidest thing I ever did. So. Here he comes. He's big and ugly and he's got a potbelly full of beer and fried chicken. Alvis Rankin. Rank Old Uncle Al. He steps into the box. Smiles at me like it's a social event. The man don't know but one thing. He knows how to hit a baseball. I throw a fastball inside, try to back him off the plate. Ball screams by, cuts the corner, ump shoots his hand out, strike one. Rankin giggles. Until the day I die, I will not know why that man giggled. He stands his ground, too. So, next ball...and this is the ironic bit...next pitch is my mistake. It's soft and square and rolls over the plate like a Cadillac down Main Street. But Rank Old Uncle Al swings over the ball, strike two. Now we start this old game, I toss 'em, Rankin fouls 'em off. Finally, I think, okay. This man intends to take my perfect game away. I will not allow it. I will throw my best pitch. It's gonna be fast and clean and lethal as grandma's twat. And that's the pitch I threw. I get goose-bumped thinking about that pitch. Only one little problem with it. Rankin took it downtown. Picked up the halter-top in row three on his way.

And that was my imperfect game. I was no-decisioned on that game. The game of my life and I'm not even the pitcher of record.

MOON: When I wrote *The Rowdy Heavens*, I was nine-teen and so frail that the wind could knock me over. I was pimpled and pale. Asthmatic. I smelled badly. But one day I sat down and wrote this line: *for he was perfect in the rowdy heavens.* Four hours later I had fifty pages. I went out and drank deeply. I saw a creature of such exquisite beauty that men grew faint and crawled under rocks. I was not to be denied. I was not to be denied.

GARY: Then Rank Old Uncle Al come along and tore up your poem.

> (MOON *and* GARY *seem to have newfound resolution*)

MOON: Let's get back to it.

GARY: Yeah.

> (GARY *hunches over the keyboard expectantly;* MOON *wanders about the room, trying to summon a line, but nothing is forthcoming*)

MOON: Um...I don't suppose any piece of Popeye rhetoric springs to mind? Something of a poetic nature that we might incorporate?

GARY: Popeye talked mostly about baseball.

MOON: What about the lepers and holy man?

GARY: What about them?

MOON: Are they the names of baseball teams? The St. Louis Lepers, the Hoboken Holy Men?

GARY: Oh, right. Well, sometimes you had to think about it pretty hard, but the things Popeye said were usually about baseball.

MOON: Well, just toss one out as an example. It might inspire us in some way.

GARY: Okay. How about, um...oh, this one's kind of poetic.

MOON: Fine.

GARY: Never throw the changer to a stranger. I like that one.

MOON: How profound.

GARY: You get it?

MOON: Never throw the changer to a stranger. Words to live by.

GARY: I don't think it would work too good in the poem, though.

MOON: How edifying to witness your burgeoning critical faculties. Well, Popeye crapped out in a big way.

GARY: You're making this seem a lot harder than it really is.

MOON: Am I, indeed?

GARY: Say one thing in poetry and you'll be over the hump. If you really don't believe there's such a thing as love, say that. But say it in poetry. Go.

MOON: *The moon's reflection on the water, foolish folk with fear and rakes.*

GARY: Does that mean there's no such thing as love?

MOON: Type away. Lord only knows what it means, but it stinks of poetry.

(GARY *types*)

Actually, it's none too shabby.

GARY: Not too goddamn shabby at all.

MOON: Alright, I'm on track. Now don't tell me any rhymes. Just sit quietly. Wait. Wait. *Foolish folk with fear and rakes, they take...*

GARY: Internal rhyme.

MOON: *They take a stab at a moon that laughs, and shimmies like a...*fat girl, obviously, but I can't say fat girl...

GARY: Porker.

MOON: *Shimmies like a question mark made of flesh...flesh...meshed...hearts...fused...hearts lowing, sounding...like a chord on a...piano.*

(*They wait*)

Piss on it! What was it Johnny Keats said? *If poetry comes not as naturally as leaves to a tree, it had better not come at all.* Well stated, Johnny, you consumptive little poofter!

GARY: Come on.

MOON: I'm stuck. Not a sausage in the old bean, mate.

David Fox as Moon and Michael Hogan as Gary in the Canadian Stage Company/Citadel Theatre production. Photo by Ed Ellis

Ah well. Sometimes the magic works, sometimes all one can do is get blind roaring drunk. Advisable strategy for young poets, Kennelly. Slake the thirst of the inner, illiterate beast. Animate the anima.

GARY: You want a suggestion?

MOON: Suggest, son, suggest.

GARY: Popeye used to tell that story about the people poking in the water, trying to fish out the moon. That was the end of it, though. Here's how it started. This fellow seen the whole family all scared because there's a sword hanging from the ceiling. I believe it was his prospective in-laws.

MOON: This sounds familiar.

GARY: Goddamn sword dangling right there from the ceiling, this whole family cowering in the corner. And the fellow says, hell, why don't you take the damn thing down? They say *good idea*. And this fellow says, shit, you are the most foolish people I ever seen. And I'm not gonna marry your daughter no matter how spectacular her boobies are.

MOON: Yes, yes.

GARY: So he says, the fellow says, come to think of it, those titties are mighty fine, so I'm going to give you one more chance. I'm gonna wander the face of this earth until I find some people more stupid than you-all. Good luck, they say. So he wanders and wanders until he finds these peasants trying to fish the moon's reflection out of the water. Using rakes, just like in your poetry. And he says, congratulations, you have out-dummied my future in-laws.

MOON: Well told, Garibaldi.

GARY: So if I were you, I'd think about putting in something else about that. Maybe about the sword.

MOON: The sword of Damocles.

GARY: Hmm?

MOON: Feasting, drinking and whoring while a sword hung by a hair over his head. Quite right, my boy. There is something there. *Hung by a hair*.

GARY: Is this poetry?

MOON: Type away.

GARY: *Hung by a hair*.

MOON: Lawler used twine.

GARY: Twine?

MOON: Ordinary twine such as one finds in any kitchen drawer. I wouldn't have thought it would be strong enough, but it seems to have done the trick. Mind you, Lawler only weighed seventy-odd pounds or something like that.

GARY: You're getting off the track, man.

MOON: It's so pitiful, son. The man uses kitchen twine and doesn't even bother to switch off the telly. Do you know why Lawler did it? Likely because there was nothing to watch on the telly. Seen it before, he tells himself, and so, having nothing better to do, he goes to his drawer, gets some twine... My sweet Jesus. Twine.

GARY: Could be he thought it wouldn't work. There's plenty of ways are surefire. There's things you can buy in any drugstore for under ten dollars kill you deader than a doorknob.

MOON: No, he knew it would work. He could have hanged himself with a hair. And dangled over our heads as we feasted, drank and whored.

GARY: You waste good poetry, Moon.

MOON: Come again?

GARY: You're saying good stuff, you know, but you're wasting it with all this feeling sorry for Old Man Lawler. You didn't even like the man.

MOON: I see. Wasting it.

GARY: You're just spouting it off into the air. Put it down on the paper.

MOON: Why don't you just help yourself to whatever poetry I spew?

GARY: Dangled over our heads. Dangling. Gangly. Dancing.

MOON: Whatever are you doing?

GARY: Transmogrification, man. I love that shit.

MOON: You wouldn't know a transmogrification if you stubbed your toe on it.

GARY: Dancing gangly overhead.

MOON: Dancing gangly overhead?

GARY: You could put *hung by a hair, dancing gangly overhead*.

MOON: You could, if you cared to.

GARY: Want to?

MOON: Oh, why not. It's not the worst line of verse I've ever heard.

GARY: (*types*) Okay, okay, here's the thing. Are we talking about a sword or what? I know you started out talking about this sword belongs to Damo-whatever but then you started talking about Old Man Lawler and I don't believe you've let up.

MOON: That's a little secret of the poet's trade. Don't let them know for certain what it is you're talking about. It makes them feel superior.

GARY: So we won't say for sure.

MOON: Just so. Let's simply say that whatever is dangling is lean and sharp. You see? And I've just had another thought, we are soon to re-introduce the word, *keen*, adding a third meaning to that already linguistically freighted word.

GARY: You're going great guns now, man.

MOON: *Sharp, lean, keened by...*

GARY: By what?

MOON: Obviously if I knew I would have said.

GARY: A stone.

MOON: This is not an instruction manual on sabre maintenance.

GARY: It's how you sharpen things. You're not necessarily talking about a sabre, but you sort of talk about a sabre but you really mean, you know, something more general.

MOON: Are you suggesting we employ the sharpening stone as a metaphor?

GARY: Bingo, first shot out of the box. Metaphor.

MOON: You've stumbled blindly into a fertile field, young Nimrod. I shall indeed employ the stones, but I shall attach to them the adjective *sorry*.

GARY: Sorry?

MOON: *Sorry stones.* Type away.

GARY: I don't know, man.

MOON: I am the poet! You are simply the typist.

GARY: What in the world have stones got to be sorry about?

MOON: If you don't shut your gob and type the following two words, *sorry* and *stones,* I shall fetch Johnny Keats and beat you to a pulp.

GARY: Okay, okay.

MOON: You've done everything in your power to thwart the invention of poetry today. You've called out rhymes, you've refused to type what I've dictated, you've given me the witch's tit to suckle. It is a testament to my artistry that I've managed as well as I have.

GARY: I beg your pardon. I'll just sit here and won't say a word.

MOON: That was what I had in mind.

GARY: Stuck for an idea?

MOON: Not at all. My mind teems. I pluck the fruits of my imagination sparingly, savouring the nectar.

GARY: 'Cause if you need an idea, I got a few.

MOON: Yes, I'm sure you do. A few Popeye-isms pounded into rhyming couplets. *Never toss the rubba at a man named Bubba.*

GARY: Just a few ideas, that's all.

MOON: I need no help, thank you. I have spied the answer. I've located the kernel, the nub of this little bit of work. Yes. We must speak of death.

GARY: Death? You barely got us born.

MOON: Don't try to understand, Kennelly. Type away. We have arrived, poetically speaking, at death.

GARY: You trying to tell me that's all there is? That's the whole ball of wax right there?

MOON: Indeed. Death is upon us.

GARY: I tell you, man, I think you better get some bright spots into this thing here.

MOON: Bright spots?

GARY: Shit, yes. I mean, didn't you ever have any fun? Lord, things get bleak from time to time, but it never was nothing but bleak, you know? How about getting your ashes hauled? That's fun.

Fishing is fun. How many fellows do you think get born and die and never catch a solitary fish in between? Who the fuck would want to read a poem where life is nothing but getting born and dying? Hell, man, we got that. We got that right outside the window. So I'm saying, back off of Big Boy Death. 'Cause I want to hear about cat-fish and pussies.

MOON: That is it. That is it, once and for all and for always. I am renouncing my position of poet. The last of the Celtic bards is no more. We were always a vastly underappreciated crew. No one shall mourn our passing. I shall forthwith drink myself into a quiet and gentle grave, and never again shall a line of verse spring from these pale, pale lips.

GARY: It was just a suggestion.

MOON: I'm giving up brushing my hair and teeth. Never again shall I clean under my fingernails. I shall live on a diet of locusts and wild honey.

GARY: Just calm down.

MOON: I'm exhilarated, Kennelly. To finally be freed of the bondage of poetry. A great load has been lifted from these shoulders. I pledge my allegiance to this stuff here. (*drinks*)

GARY: You're behaving like a little kid.

MOON: Because I have regained my innocence.

GARY: Look, man, I'm sorry.

MOON: No, no. You were right. Quite right.

GARY: Maybe death is all there is.

MOON: No. Go ahead. Please, don't let me stop you. Write about a nice fish. That's what is called for, I see that now. You were absolutely correct. (*drinks*)

GARY: You're going to drink it all. Give me that bottle.

MOON: I give you fair warning. It interferes with the poetic sensibilities.

GARY: Give it over.

MOON: Maintaining, are we? That does sound much better than being drunk.

(MOON *hands over the bottle.* GARY *drinks*)

GARY: This was your idea, you know. Don't forget that.

MOON: Look, I don't remember —

GARY: And if you don't remember it's because you blacked out, and if you blacked out you got a yes on one of the twenty questions and I'm here to tell you you got maybe fifteen fucking yesses and you are as hopeless an alkie as anyone.

MOON: Piss off.

GARY: I'd like to help you write a poem because I know how bad you feel.

MOON: How could you possibly know?

GARY: How could I know?

MOON: Look, mate, if you know so bleeding much, you don't need me. You just carry on. Write the fucking poem yourself.

GARY: You keep up this business, Jack, I may just do that.

MOON: Consider the business up-kept, bucko.

GARY: Alright.

MOON: Alright?

GARY: You think you're the only one in the world can write poetry, you got one more damn thing coming. You're the last of the Celtic Bards, well I say, I don't even know what league they play in. Any old body can write poetry. So I'm gonna.

MOON: Be my guest.

GARY: You just pipe down. Drink your booze. Hopeless alkie.

MOON: If nothing else, this experience will give you a renewed appreciation of me.

GARY: Don't hold your breath. (*types for a long moment*)

MOON: There. Thought we'd feel better, didn't we, but there's a vague sense of dissatisfaction. A kind of overwhelming sadness.

GARY: Didn't notice that. Feels okay. (*types again*)

MOON: It can be almost sexual, can't it? But let me tell you, the climax never comes. The poetical orgasm is a mythical beast.

GARY: Will you please keep quiet?

MOON: A thousand pardons. I failed to see the "Poet At Work" sign.

       (*they sit quietly for a few moments*)

Bogged down?

GARY: I'm trying to decide between two words.

MOON: Oh, thought of two words, have you? My advice is, select the one that's easier to spell.

GARY: I'm trying to describe a lizard.

MOON: A lizard? How could you possibly be wanting to describe a lizard? There's nothing even vaguely reptilian!

GARY: The lizard is going to be a what-you-call-it.

MOON: A metaphor?

GARY: Correct-a-mundo.

MOON: Kennelly is going to employ a metaphor. How clever. Pray tell, for what is the lizard a metaphor?

GARY: Just a plain old metaphor.

MOON: Garden variety metaphor, you say?

GARY: That's right. Maybe you use some fancy metaphors, but I'm just starting out.

MOON: I can see it now. The doctoral thesis. The Use of Reptilian and Amphibious Analogy in the Poetry of Washed-up —

GARY: Hey, now.

MOON: *Washed-up* baseball player and poet, Gary Kennelly.

GARY: Hush up, Moon. If you want to start talking washed-up —

MOON: Yes?

GARY: I'm just saying.

MOON: You're always saying *I'm just saying* but you never say anything.

GARY: You ought to try listening some time. I'm just saying that I ain't read about you in any recent issues of *People* magazine.

MOON: My reputation is secure. I've been nominated
    for the Nobel, Kennelly. Not this year. Some
    years back, at the height of my creative powers.
    Mind you, there was some politicking going on
    within the jury, and the award was given to some
    Norwegian with cancer.

> (GARY *looks up suddenly; he studies* MOON
> *and types a word or two*)

Didn't cheer him up much, I must say. Gloomiest
    mook I ever saw, that Norwegian.

> (GARY *studies* MOON *again*)

MOON: What the hell are you staring at?

GARY: You have a lumpy head.

MOON: I have a lumpy head.

GARY: I never noticed it before.

MOON: Everyone's got a lumpy head. It comes from
    being born. That's quite the little hole to pop out
    of, my lad. It's bound to affect skull structure.

GARY: I guess that's so. (*types a word or two*)

MOON: Do you have something about my head in
    there?

GARY: Not about your head, exactly. No, sir.

MOON: You've gone from lizards to my head in such a
    short time?

GARY: Lizard was a metaphor.

MOON: Yes, of course. It had slipped my mind.

GARY: How do you spell that word *infidelity*?

MOON: Oh, don't spell infidelity, Gary. It's an awful word. A sludgy earthbound wormeaten word. It has no business in a bit of poetry. Fortunately for you, the muses have spoken to me once again. Listen to this lovely line that they have granted me. *The stars scattered like a madman's fancies*. How about that then?

GARY: I-n-f-e-d —

MOON: Shut up. Write as follows, *the stars scattered like a madman's fancies*.

GARY: I can't.

MOON: Why the hell not?

GARY: I'm kind of into specifics here.

MOON: What could be more specific than the stars?

GARY: Look, I'll try to work the line in. But right now I got my hands full with these other things.

MOON: Lizards and my lumpy skull. What the Jesus kind of poem is this?

GARY: I don't know.

MOON: Well, I know. It's my poem. It's my epic! It's about heaven and the stars and being popped out of a little hole in the middle of all that. So I say, what's needed here is a line about the stars, and I say that the stars are scattered like a madman's fancies, which is a brilliant bloody line as anybody can tell you, and you are just the typist, so type!

GARY: Just let me finish this bit here.

MOON: This bit about my head?

GARY: This bit about me and Jocelyn.

MOON: Don't put anything about Jocelyn in the poem, Gary. It's volunteered information.

GARY: It's just some stuff about some of the shit we went through. That's all.

MOON: Is there anything about how she was in bed? Write about her pear-shaped breasts, Kennelly. Write about her golden honey-pot.

GARY: Watch your mouth.

MOON: Oh, if you're going to rip it out, rip it out. No half measures! Write about every foul-smelling orifice and every withered appendage you shoved up it.

GARY: Why are you so fucking mad?

MOON: Because you ruined my poem.

GARY: I didn't ruin nothing. And it's not yours.

MOON: I left you with a thing of crystalline beauty. The words hovered in the welkin. In the brief time you've laboured at it, you have brutally hauled it down to earth, and are at present composing a ditty to your ex-wife's sad and sagging dugs.

GARY: You don't know what I'm writing and you don't care.

MOON: This has gone far enough! (*rushes over to the table, scoops up the typewriter, then over to the window*)

Take one step towards me and I throw the machine out the window! I have saved poetry! Poetry was being molested at the hands of this Philistine but I intervened and —

> (GARY *gets up abruptly and marches toward his coat*)

You'll thank me, Kennelly! Your heart was about to get mangled to morsels!

> (GARY *rifles through his jacket pocket, extracts a pencil. He crosses over to the table and sits down. He begins to write in longhand.* MOON *watches him for a moment or two, then concedes.* MOON *brings back the*

> *typewriter, places it on the table.* MOON
> *whispers first to the machine)*

MOON: Don't worry, darling, it will be over soon.

Alright, Kennelly, do the dirty deed.

> (GARY *continues typing steadily.* MOON
> *crosses over to the window and stares out)*

Yes. I do think even that brief outing into poetry land has gotten the old juices flowing. My mistake was alcoholic consumption. Entirely your fault, Kennelly. A solemn pledge means nothing to you. But you got me drunk, so, of course, nothing happened. As Popeye Finlayson would say, inspiration plus consumption equals constipation. But I can feel it. Yes, it's there, coursing through the old veins, merrily skipping on a river of whiskey. Poetry. I love the old marm. Not only that, I've been granted a vision. The epic and ethereal thrust of that little ditty — by the way, how's it coming along ?

GARY: Okay.

MOON: Do you want a sandwich or anything?

GARY: No, thank you.

MOON: If you get a little peckish, just shout.

At any rate, I've been granted — thank you,

Sisters — a grand vision. An epic. Perhaps my masterwork. Nine poems, each corresponding to a planet. But I'll avoid the usual doggerel and dongswallow. I mean, what exactly is warlike about Mars? Some myopic Druid spied the thing, noted it was pinkish, decided it flowed with blood. Pretty fucking simple-minded, if you ask me. Or Pluto. People are very harsh on Pluto. Why? Because it's far away. Not if you're on Pluto, mate. No. I reckon Pluto's a nice enough place. Lots of snow. Lots of soft, white snow. You just get drunk and — (*regards the bottle in his hand, wanders over to sit wearily on the bed*)

It's true.

GARY: Hmm?

MOON: You asked me earlier on. Kristal. Kristal the Purple Whore.

GARY: Right. (*continues working at a steady pace, not really listening*)

MOON: I had her kneel in front of me and stare into my eyes. For an hour. Thirty-seven fifty it cost me. Where on God's dear earth did she come up with that amount? She assesses her value at the rate of thirty-seven fifty per hour, although I gather she assumes the two-and-a-half dollar tip. If you had exact change, however, I warrant she'd bear you no grudge.

So, for thirty-seven fifty, Kristal kneeled in front of me and stared into my eyes. Look into my eyes, I told her. Look into me. Because there used to be so much there. Now, there's nothing. Look into my eyes. Tell me if you see something. Anything. She looked into my eyes for an hour — thirty-seven fifty's worth — and then she said, jeez, she said, you have cute eyes.

GARY: Why don't you just shut up? I mean, keep your mouth shut. Don't say anything.

MOON: This is my bloody room. I don't have to take orders from some functional illiterate banging away on the typewriter making a mockery of all I keep holy.

GARY: You keep jackshit holy, Moon. Now shut up.

MOON: If you were possessed of any intelligence at all, Kennelly, you would encourage me to speak. It's the only bloody poetry you'll ever come close to.

GARY: I'm encouraging you to shut up.

MOON: Dylan was a great poet who loved to talk. Brendan was a great talker who loved to write poetry. I am that rarest of things, a great talker and a great poet.

GARY: A great talker. Don't make me laugh. You don't talk. At least, you don't talk to people. You talk *at* them. You just talk and don't care if anybody is listening or has anything to say back.

MOON: Indeed?

GARY: Who do you think sits with you when you're drunk and start blubbering and talking about your son? You never even noticed who that was, Moon. It was me. You never talked to me. You don't know the first damn thing about me.

MOON: Alright. Tell me something. Tell me...tell me about your daughter.

GARY: She got leukemia.

MOON: No. Not that daughter. Your other daughter. You had twins, only one had leukemia.

GARY: Melody? She's shaved her head bald. She has tattoos. She has a tattoo of a snake crawling across her belly. She lives in a terrible, terrible place. She's a whore.

MOON: Alright. Tell me about the other one.

GARY: She died.

MOON: Yes. I see. I know. I see.

GARY: Can you believe that? What the hell kind of deal is that? Hey, Moon. Mr. Great Talker. Explain it to me. You explain to me a God that would make a little girl like that — perfect, man, perfect —

and then fill her with disease that eats away at her until she is nothing but skin and bones and black eyes and no hair and... Explain it to me.

MOON: I can't, son.

GARY: That's why I became a Born Again. 'Cause I wanted to talk to that bugger. Say to Him, *hey*! Explain it to me. That's all I want.

MOON: Even if it were explained, what good would it be?

GARY: Explain it to me!

MOON: She's dead, son. But your other daughter...

GARY: She's a whore.

MOON: You cannot leave her, you must not abandon her.

GARY: *Whosoever diggeth a pit shall fall there-in. He that rolleth a stone, it will return upon him.*

MOON: No. *Come now, and let us reason together, saith the Lord; though your sins be as scarlet, they shall be white as snow.*

GARY: You big faker, Moon. You believe in God. You believe in the Goody Two-Shoes God. I believe in the God that fucking killed my daughter!

MOON: God did not kill your daughter. A disease killed your daughter. A loathsome little disease that eats away life.

GARY: Sometimes I just want to tear their fucking heads off.

MOON: Who's this now?

GARY: Them alkies in Assholes Anonymous. 'Cause sometime I might mention, you know, I think I got my bad drinking problem when Melanie died. And they say, that's just an excuse. Don't call it an excuse. *This* is an excuse. This is an excuse for living, all of us huddled, hiding, in this church basement, pretending that we're so fucking happy. Bullshit!

MOON: I think their point is that drinking often deflects, you see, from...

GARY: Just an excuse for drinking? That's what my little girl's life amounts to, an excuse for drinking? I'll tear their fucking throats out, man. Hey! (*starts to type frantically*)

MOON: You're getting yourself into a state, son.

GARY: (*continues to pound on the typewriter*)*Golden hair. Singing songs while she skips the rope. Laughs at the cat chasing its own tail.*

MOON: Don't, son.

GARY: I can put her on the paper.

MOON: You can't, you can't. (*moves towards* GARY *and the typewriter*)

GARY: Back off. When I'm done, you do it, Moon. Put in about God. Put in about your wife and how much you loved her. Put in about Hamish, Moon. Put in about how Old Man Lawler's hanging himself has made you so damn scared you can't sleep at night...

MOON: No! (*tears the sheet out of the carriage, begins to tear it into tiny pieces*)

GARY: What the fuck are you doing?

MOON: It's for your own good.

> (GARY *crawls over on his hands and knees and sifts through the pieces of paper*)

How do you think I ended up here? I tore out my heart and put it on paper and now I no longer have it. Do you want to end up like me? Empty?

GARY: Yes.

MOON: I haven't been out of this hotel in eight years. I haven't changed out of my bathrobe in almost six.

GARY: And what do you think, like I got a social life? (*looks at the pieces of paper with despair*)

Words. Now it's just stupid words all over the floor.

MOON: It never was anything but words, Gary.

GARY: It was a poem. It was a damn nice poem and it

made me feel better. You had no right to tear up my poem.

MOON: It was my poem as well. A poet has a right to tear up his own creation.

GARY: The first part maybe was yours. The part I didn't understand. You should have just torn up that. You shouldn't have torn up my part of the poem. (*pause*) Moon?

MOON: Yes?

GARY: I have the means, Moon.

MOON: What?

GARY: In my room. I have the means. I have the means covered about four ways, Moon. And that was before you told me about the snow.

MOON: Oh. Those means.

GARY: I'm sorry, Moon.

MOON: Nothing to be sorry about, lad. It's often prudent to, um, have the means. But perhaps you won't need them, now...now that you've discovered poetry.

GARY: You tore up the poem.

MOON: Think of this as an introduction to the often brutal editing process.

GARY: Huh?

MOON: We have only to begin again.

GARY: Oh, no. I'm too tired.

MOON: You lack the stamina to be a poet, Kennelly.
        Sleep takes a back seat when the Muse is upon us.

GARY: I don't think I can.

MOON: Rewriting. That's the secret of it, buck. Not
        bunging down words. Sifting through the dross
        and finding the truly lustrous words. Look. *Keen-
        ing*. That's a lovely word. We'll keep that one.
        Here's another. *Blonde*. Pedestrian. Dull. Still...a
        good word, all the same. We must have
        blondness in this poem. Here's another word.

> (MOON *picks up a tiny bit of paper; he has
> difficulty making it out and hands it to*
> GARY)

GARY: *Infidelity*. Not a good word.

MOON: It's all here. Poetry.

GARY: I might be willing to try one more time. But...

MOON: But?

GARY: Well, I've decided that I think poems should
        rhyme. At least sometimes. So, if I shout out a
        rhyme, I don't want you jumping all over my
        case.

MOON: Yes. Well, similarly, if I conjure up a fine line like *the stars scattered like a mad man's fancies*, I don't want it turfed out on some trumped-up charge of lacking specificity.

GARY: Yeah. Okay.

MOON: Do we have a done deal?

GARY: Done deal.

> (*They shake hands and climb to their feet.*
> GARY *re-papers the machine*)

GARY: Ready, Moon?

MOON: Ready.

GARY: (*begins to type*) *We came from the hills* —

MOON: *And were heavengoing.*

GARY: And were heavengoing.

> (*curtain*)
>
> *The End*

Amigo's Blue Guitar

Joan MacLeod

Sander's life is given meaning when he chooses
to sponsor a Salvadoran refugee for his
sociology class. He never really thinks Elias will
make it to Canada, and when he does, Sander
and his family must learn what it means and
feels like to be a refugee, and how to best relate
to someone who has endured such intense
personal grief. The warmth and humour of the
fully-human characters invites us to embrace the
situation, be moved by it, threatened by it, and
to consider how we would react.

*...theatre of exceptional power....[A] subtle, often
funny and ultimately moving play.*

MACLEANS'S

Memories of You

Wendy Lill

The life of Elizabeth Smart pivoted on a turbulent affair that produced one book and four children. When her youngest daughter, the resentful and drug-ridden Rose comes to visit, an explosion of emotion between mother and daughter erupts, as well as an explosion of memories for Smart.

Memories is beautifully written... Everything about it reaches for the ecstatic — its pleasure, its sensuality and its pain. Memories is a courageous and profoundly moving play...

ROBERT ENRIGHT, CBC RADIO

Fire

Paul Ledoux and David Young

Inspired by the lives of cousins Jerry Lee Lewis
and Jimmy Lee Swaggart, *Fire* tells the story of
two Razorback, Arkansas brothers who follow
different branches of the same road of pride,
lust, and greed. Cale sells his soul to rock and
roll, Herchel to TV evangelism. Both love Molly,
who loves both of them. *Fire* ignites with the
passion of love, Jesus, and music of rock 'n roll
and gospel.

*This show has drawn large audiences because the
story is so powerful and so plausible... Fire is a
dynamic piece of theatre...*

THE GLOBE AND MAIL

Midnight Madness

Dave Carley

Wesley and Anna haven't seen each other since
they both quit high school years ago. Their
reasons for quitting were as different as they
were, or so it might seem, until they discover
plenty they never knew about each other in the
bed department of Bloom's furniture store.

*"A gentle little comedy...a play that will delight and
touch audiences for years to come."*

TORONTO STAR